CIVIL RIGHTS

The Long Struggle

Eileen Lucas

—Issues in Focus—

Enslow Publishers, Inc.

44 Fadem Road   PO Box 38
Box 699   Aldershot
Springfield, NJ 07081   Hants GU12 6BP
USA   UK

Library of Congress Cataloging-in-Publication Data

Lucas, Eileen.
    Civil rights, the long struggle / Eileen Lucas.
        p. cm. — (Issues in focus)
    Includes bibliographical references and index.
    Summary: Focuses on the history of civil rights for African
  Americans from the founding of the nation to the Million Man March.
    ISBN 0-89490-729-8
    1. Civil rights—United States—History—Juvenile literature.
    2. Afro-Americans—Civil rights—History—Juvenile literature.
    [1. Civil rights—History. 2. Afro-Americans—Civil rights.]
    I. Title. II. Series: Issues in focus (Hillside, N.J.)
    JC599.U5L78 1996
    323.1'196073—dc20   96-12264
                                          CIP
                                          AC

Printed in the United States of America

10 9 8 7 6 5 4 3 2 1

Photo Credits: Bettman Archives, pp. 63, 67; Library of Congress, pp. 13,
22, 42, 50, 56, 58, 71, 75, 79, 94; National Archives, pp. 15, 24, 34, 40,
48, 84 ; Stephen R. Ausmus, pp. 7, 29, 38, 73, 96.

Cover Photo: *Walworth County Week*, Dan Plutchak

Contents

1   Still in the News Today   5

2   Fundamental Rights   9

3   Precious Freedoms   17

4   Freedom—For Whom?—
  1791–1954   32

5   Cracks in the Wall—
  1954–1965   52

6   The Movement Fragments—
  1965–1968   69

7   Rights for All   77

8   Today, Tomorrow, and . . .
  One Day   92

  Chronology 100

  Chapter Notes 103

  Glossary 108

  Further Reading 110

  Index 111

1

Still in the News Today

The United States Constitution protects its citizens against abuses by the government. That is what the people who wrote it were concerned about—creating a government strong enough to provide an environment in which "life, liberty and the pursuit of happiness" could thrive, while keeping the government's power within reasonable limits. For more than two hundred years, Americans have frequently debated how well this balance between a strong government and a free people has actually been achieved.

The debate continues today. Debates over civil rights issues can be found in newspapers and magazines and on radio and television programs across the country. Is racism still such a factor in daily life that the government needs to provide special opportunities for minorities, or are such "affirmative action" programs unfair and insulting? Is violence so out of hand in low-income housing complexes known as "projects" that "gun sweeps" are a legitimate protection of residents? Or is this a gross violation of the right to protection against unreasonable search and seizure?

What about young peoples' rights in school? Can schools legally search students' desks, lockers, or personal possessions? Do students have the right to free speech in school? Where do my rights end and yours begin? Who will decide if we disagree about this?

Some people say that the very fact that we can debate these questions shows that our rights, including freedom of speech, are protected. Others point to such incidents as the 1991 beating of black motorist Rodney King by white Los Angeles police officers as evidence that, at least for some Americans, there is a gap between rights that are promised and rights that are protected.

In recent years, radio talk shows have been one of the outlets for loud voices raised in anger exclaiming that the American government has in fact become oppressive and invasive. G. Gordon Liddy, a widely listened-to radio talk show host, "told his listeners that if federal agents invade their homes, they should shoot at their heads because of the agents' protective vests."[1] Another talk show host explained how to use nylon rope to hang legislators. Some of the people listening to these shows were stockpiling arms and ammunition, preparing to fight not a foreign invader, but the government of the United States, perceived by them as having become the enemy. In the spring of 1995, President Bill Clinton criticized some of these "loud and angry voices in America today," saying, "They spread hate; they leave the impression, by their very words, that violence is acceptable."[2]

There are many people in our society who think that there is a gap between rights that are promised and rights that are protected.

In a poll taken on April 27, 1995, for *Time* magazine, 52 percent of the 600 adults polled felt that the federal government had become so powerful that it posed a threat to the rights and freedoms of its citizens. Yet, at the same time, 68 percent felt that the federal government should be able to spy on antigovernment groups in order to monitor their activities.[3]

It seems that Americans are still struggling to find the right balance between a government strong enough to protect itself but not so strong as to interfere with the rights of its citizens. The story of civil rights in America continues to be written every day. Who knows, you may be writing the next chapter. Will you be prepared?

2

Fundamental Rights

The idea that people have rights is an ancient one. The concept goes back thousands of years, to the days of the ancient Greeks and Romans. Almost since the beginning of government, there have been people who claimed for themselves and others certain basic rights.

What exactly are civil rights? A right is something that a person is entitled to. Human rights are things that people are entitled to as human beings, such as, perhaps, the right not to be tortured or enslaved. Civil rights are those things that a person is entitled to because of his or her status as a citizen or as a member of a society. In other words, civil rights are the rights of citizens. A civil right is described by author Reginald Wilson as ". . . a fundamental right that assures equal worth and dignity to each and every member of society."[1]

Nearly every group of people within American society has had their civil rights violated due to prejudice and discrimination at one time or another. For example, signs reading "No Irish Need Apply" could be found in many shops and businesses in the late 1800s and early 1900s. There were also many Japanese Americans who lost their homes and businesses during World War II simply because of their ancestry.

For many Americans, however, the term "civil rights" often brings to mind equality between black citizens and white citizens. While other members of society have been, and continue to be, involved in civil rights issues, much of this book discusses the progress of African Americans in the civil rights movement. The story of that fight for justice dramatically illustrates the fight for civil rights in the United States.

In this country, civil rights are established by laws, court decisions on what the laws mean, and the Constitution, particularly in the amendments known as the Bill of Rights. They indicate what individuals should be allowed to do, or not do, and they restrict what the government can do in relation to its people. They are extensions of human rights.

Few, if any, rights are absolute. Rights can be limited by responsibilities—if you don't fulfill your responsibilities, you may be forced to give up your rights. Adults have the right to bear children, but they also have many responsibilities in relation to those children.

Your rights may also be limited by other peoples' rights. You have the right to express your complaints against a fellow citizen, but that citizen also has the right to be free from being hurt by you.

People in authority may say that we give up our rights when we do something wrong. We may lose our freedom if we commit a crime; the authorities may even decide that we lose our right to life if the crime committed is serious enough.

Finally, people in authority may choose to ignore our rights for other reasons, such as, perhaps, "national security." In times of war or instability, individual rights may be considered secondary to those of the government.

The Development of Rights

Throughout history, there have been a number of approaches to the philosophy of rights. Some of them have called upon "natural law." This philosophy states that people have some basic rights simply because they are humans, at the top of the creations of God or nature. It is "natural" for them to have certain rights.

Others have claimed that it is useful for society to grant individuals certain freedoms because it makes them better citizens. This is the "utilitarian" school of thought.

One of the earliest documents guaranteeing the rights of citizens was the Magna Carta, signed by King John of England in 1215. With this document, the noblemen of England forced their king to accept that there were certain limits to his power. In 1649 the king of England was overthrown, and the people demanded a constitution that would define the limits of the power of government. This power would be further restricted during the next several decades.

An American Bill of Rights

There were already English colonists in North America when the English Parliament adopted its Declaration of Rights in 1689. These colonists, and those that followed,

11

believed that these rights applied to them too. Thus, when Parliament tried to force them in the 1760s to pay increased taxes while at the same time denying them a voice in that body, it was called "taxation without representation," a violation of colonists' rights. One of their most memorable protests was to throw tea overboard in Boston Harbor rather than pay a tax on it. The British government responded by closing Boston Harbor and installing troops in colonists' homes in that town. The colonists called together a Continental Congress to decide how to react.

On October 14, 1774, they issued a Declaration of Rights. This said that they were no longer bound by Parliament or the king when their rights were limited. During May of 1776, the Second Continental Congress called on the colonies to adopt individual constitutions and set up governments of their own. On July 4, 1776, by signing the Declaration of Independence, the colonies formally broke with "the British Crown" and prepared to fight for their independence.

At the end of the revolution, Britain signed a treaty that "acknowledges the said United States . . . to be free, sovereign and independent States."[2] These United States were only very loosely united under a document called the Articles of Confederation.

Under these Articles, the country was governed by a group of leaders chosen from each state. This Congress was subject to neither president nor king, and it had very little power to act. It could not raise money through taxes and could not control trade between the various states. After a few years of this, it became clear that the new country was in danger of falling apart, and that

PUBLISHED BY CURRIER & IVES   Entered according to act of Congress in the year 1876 by Currier & Ives, in the Office of the Librarian of Congress at Washington.   123 NASSAU ST. NEW YORK
THOMAS JEFFERSON.   ROGER SHERMAN.   BENJAMIN FRANKLIN.   ROBERT R. LIVINGSTON.   JOHN ADAMS.

THE DECLARATION COMMITTEE.

THOMAS JEFFERSON of Virginia, JOHN ADAMS of Massachusetts, BENJAMIN FRANKLIN of Pennsylvania, ROGER SHERMAN of Connecticut, ROBERT R. LIVINGSTON of New York, were appointed June 11th 1776 a Committee to draw up a Declaration in accordance with the resolution offered in Congress June 7th 1776, by Richard Henry Lee, of Virginia, (who being suddenly called to the bedside of his sick wife, was unable to serve personally upon the Committee,) the Declaration was prepared by the Chairman, Thomas Jefferson, and with few alterations reported by the Committee to the Congress July 1st and at mid-day July 4th 1776, the Thirteen Colonies were declared, Free and Independent States, under the name of the United States of America.

The Declaration of Independence was drawn up after the British limited the rights of American colonists. Over two hundred years later, Americans still struggle to find balance between a strong government and fundamental civil rights.

something better was needed. On May 25, 1787, representatives from the states met in Philadelphia to begin the process of correcting and reforming the Articles. What they ended up with was a whole new constitution, representing a brand-new form of government. It granted Congress the power to tax and to regulate trade. It listed some rights that American

13

citizens would enjoy. One of these was the right of *habeas corpus*, meaning that a person, or literally, the body of a person, must be presented, or freed, if there is no just cause for holding them in connection with a crime. Another right that was guaranteed was the right to trial by jury.

The Constitution that the delegates accepted and sent to the states to be approved was remarkable—but it was not perfect. It had been achieved by a process of debate and compromise. One of the major issues on which the Constitution compromised was slavery. For well over a hundred years, Africans had been forcibly brought to the colonies against their will, to work on the farms and in the towns. At first they were mostly treated much like the indentured servants who were brought willingly from Europe and granted freedom after their time of service was completed. In time, however, rules that would keep African laborers in chains and force them to live and die as slaves became firmly established in American thinking. Despite the fact that thousands of African Americans fought on the American side in the Revolutionary War, and that many of the founding fathers were personally against slavery, no one took a firm stand on this issue, and it was not outlawed in the Constitution.

Most of the representatives at the Constitutional Convention felt that their compromises represented the best government that could be achieved at that time. Some of them, however, feared that the new Constitution made the government too strong. They said that it must have a bill of rights, guaranteeing certain liberties to the people. One of the strongest of these voices was that of George Mason from Virginia. In a series of essays he described his concerns and pleaded for a bill of rights.

The Bill of Rights guarantees certain liberties to all American citizens.

Others said that there were already rights given to the people in the states' constitutions and there was nothing in the federal document to take those away. These people were called Federalists. Alexander Hamilton and James Madison were among their most influential leaders.

This debate was carried on throughout the thirteen states where the Constitution had to be ratified, or accepted, by the individual lawmaking bodies, called legislatures.

Finally, from where he was serving in Paris as America's minister to France, Thomas Jefferson wrote to the Federalists and asked them to accept a bill of rights: "a bill of rights," he said, "is what the people are entitled to against every government on earth, general or particular, and what no just government should refuse or rest on inference."[3]

With the condition that amendments containing a bill of rights would follow, the Constitution was ratified (approved) by the required number of states on June 21, 1788, and legally went into effect at that time.

A president and members of Congress were elected. In the first session of Congress, James Madison introduced the amendments that would make up the Bill of Rights. They were based on statements about civil rights that were already included in many of the individual states' constitutions.

Ten amendments, which today we call the Bill of Rights, were ratified on December 15, and became part of the Constitution of the United States.[4] In the next chapter we shall explore the Bill of Rights, which has played such a vital role in American history.

3

Precious Freedoms

The Constitution and its amendments can be read in about half an hour, but you could spend the rest of your life studying what they mean and how they have been interpreted by the courts and applied by lawmakers. The courts are dependent on citizens to bring forward cases in which they think the Constitution has been violated by a law or by actions. Citizen action is a vital part of the protection of civil rights.

How the Government Works

The United States Constitution, with the Bill of Rights and additional amendments, is a description of how the government is supposed to work. It states that the government is granted authority by the people to do its job, but that the people also have certain rights. Some of the rights listed in the Constitution are very specific;

others are more general. Some have received very little attention while others are the subject of debate.

The Constitution comes from the people of the United States and can be changed by the people of the United States. It should be remembered that the Constitution applies to the relationship between the people and the government, not so much to the relationships between individuals. So, when the Constitution prohibits discrimination by the government, it does not necessarily apply to discrimination between individuals, unless the government is involved in some way.

Debates on the meaning of the Constitution often hinge on "original intent"—what the framers meant when they wrote it. This must be balanced with flexibility for changing times. The American system of government balances the decisions of the majority with protection for the rights of minorities. Thus, the power of the majority is limited.

The First Amendment

The First Amendment contains fewer than fifty words, but it says a lot in those words. It protects the rights of freedom of religion, freedom of speech for individuals and the press, and freedom of assembly and petition.

Freedom of Religion

At the time the Constitution was written, many of the nations of the world had an official church supported by the government. In many of these countries, believers of any faith other than the official one were persecuted.

This was true in England, the country from which many of the colonists had come to escape persecution. Unfortunately, many of these people were, in turn, no more tolerant than their persecutors. They created church-controlled colonies in which only one form of religious observance was allowed.

One of the exceptions to this was the colony of Rhode Island. Founded by Roger Williams, a Puritan banished from Massachusetts for his beliefs, Rhode Island was one of the few colonies that allowed freedom of worship for Jews, Catholics, Quakers, and Puritans.

The First Amendment says that the government will not declare or establish any one religion as the official religion of this country. This is known as the establishment clause. The second part of the same amendment is known as the exercise clause. It states that individuals are free to practice (exercise) or not practice any religion as they see fit without government interference. The government cannot punish someone for going to synagogue on Saturday or church on Sunday. Nor can it punish someone for not going. It is simply none of the government's business. The only time religious beliefs become the business of the government is when they result in actions that violate laws or interfere with the rights of others. For example, it is against the law to have more than one marriage partner at a time, even if a person's religious beliefs allow this (as was the case among Mormons in the 1800s).

Debate about the meaning of this amendment has led to the philosophy of the separation of church and state. There has been much discussion throughout our nation's history on this issue.

... According to a number of critics ... the Supreme Court of the United States has become neutral *against* religion. These critics point out that public places, ceremonies and offices are gradually [losing] religious reference. They further point out ... that to omit references to religion is not to teach nothing about it; it is to teach that religion is ... a matter of private but not public concern. This is not, the critics conclude, what the founders of this country intended, what the Constitution stipulates, or what most Americans want.[1]

On the other hand, "Some people interpret the First Amendment as a strict and uncrossable line. They believe that government should not support activities that could be interpreted as religious, such as prayer in schools or nativity scenes on public property."[2]

Freedom of Speech

The First Amendment also says that Congress shall make no law abridging, or infringing on, the freedom of speech or of the press. If a person knows only one of the freedoms guaranteed by the Bill of Rights, it is likely to be freedom of speech.

The founders of our nation believed that a major requirement for democracy was an informed public. Freedom to speak one's mind, and to publish one's ideas, was considered an important right.

It didn't take long for this philosophy to be tested. In 1798 Congress passed a series of laws known as the Alien and Sedition Acts. These acts arose from a fear of aliens, people from foreign countries, living in the United States. A nation less than a generation old, created by the descendants of immigrants, was now afraid of newcomers.

The purpose of the Alien and Sedition Acts was to prevent criticism of the government, which President John Adams seemed especially to fear from immigrants. Critics such as James Madison noted that Americans had rejected the idea that government officials "are the masters and not the servants of the people."[3]

The question of limits on the freedom of speech has been at the heart of many First Amendment cases over the years. Three areas in which limits have sometimes been established are: when speech causes harm to the reputation of others (this is called slander or libel); when speech presents a clear and present danger to the public or the government (such as yelling "Fire!" in a crowded theater when no fire exists); or when speech is considered obscene or in conflict with the moral values of society. Businesses also have limits on the complete right to freedom of speech. For example, it is illegal to misrepresent the ability of products to do certain things.

Sometimes people disagree about these limits on freedom of speech. Individuals such as former Supreme Court Justices Hugo Black and William Douglas, and groups such as the American Civil Liberties Union (ACLU), have consistently held that there should be few, if any, limitations on speech. Others find some expressions (such as pornography or hate-filled speech) offensive enough to require banning.

Another tricky freedom of speech debate is in regards to "symbolic expression." This involves an act, rather than a verbal or written statement, which is made to express an opinion. Sometimes symbolic expression is

The Alien and Sedition Acts limited civil rights in that they were designed to curb people's speech and to limit government criticism.

protected under the First Amendment and sometimes it is not. For example, during the Vietnam War protests, burning draft cards was found to be an illegal act because the government had a strong interest in maintaining the military. However, the right of students to wear black armbands as a sign of their feelings against the war was upheld in another Supreme Court case.

Freedom of Assembly and Petition

Americans have always been great joiners. The right to gather with people of common interest, even if that common interest is unpopular, is protected by the last part of the First Amendment. The gathering, however, must be peaceful.

Just as there are some restrictions on the freedom of speech, there are also some on the freedom of assembly. Assembled groups are subject to laws that protect the lives, liberties, and property of others. The freedom of assembly and petition includes the right to picket or march in protest as determined by the Supreme Court in 1940, as long as it is peaceful and does not interfere with the business of the place being picketed. It does not grant the right to assemble for violent or illegal purposes.

Guns for Militia and the Quartering of Troops

The Second and Third Amendments were meant to restrict the ability of the federal government from using military force against its own people.

In 1973, a federal appeals court stated "It must be remembered that the right to keep and bear arms is not a

The Bill of Rights protects the right to assemble. Here, a woman protests at an antinuclear demonstration.

right given by the United States Constitution."[4] This might surprise you if you have ever heard any of the discussion that claims citizens have a constitutional right to own a gun. According to the federal appeals court's interpretation of the Constitution, the Second Amendment does not prohibit the government from regulating the private use of certain kinds of guns, such as assault weapons, or even from prohibiting the private possession of some guns, such as machine guns or sawed-off shotguns.

What the Second Amendment states is that the people have a right to bear arms (have guns) so that a militia can be maintained. It does not say anything about a right to own guns outside the context of a state militia. At the writing of this amendment, there was no police force in America, and no large permanent military force. Citizens were expected to protect themselves and to be ready to serve the country as soldiers with their own weapons.

Today we have a professionally trained and equipped police force and military. Many citizens feel that certain limits on weapons in the hands of private citizens are appropriate. In an era of guided missiles and nuclear weapons, private citizens could hardly be expected to protect the nation from foreign invaders. Guns offer only limited protection from criminals, these people would argue. They might also argue that guns often present more of a danger to the gun owner and other innocent people than to criminals.

Other Americans disagree, claiming that the Second Amendment *does* guarantee the rights of individuals to own guns. The National Rifle Association (NRA) keeps its members informed of any actions by the government that it sees as limiting this right.

The Third Amendment refers back to a time when the British government punished the colonists by making them "quarter" troops; in other words, forcing them to have soldiers live with them in their homes. It is not something that American people today worry much about. However, the Third Amendment gives further emphasis to the fact that civilians, in the form of the president and the Congress, do have authority over the military.

Search and Seizure

The Fourth through Eighth Amendments expand on the constitutional guarantees of just enforcement of laws and fair treatment for people accused of crimes.

During the years before the American Revolution, the colonists saw themselves as victims of violations of their right to privacy within their homes. "Writs of assistance" allowed British soldiers to enter their homes at any time, and to search for and take anything they wanted. To prevent this from happening in the future, the Fourth Amendment was created. It requires that (in most cases) a document called a warrant be issued. The warrant must clearly state what is being looked for and why. It must be presented before a person's home is searched. In order to further prevent authorities from making unreasonable searches, the Supreme Court decided in 1914 that any material found in an illegal search cannot be used as evidence in court. This gives the Fourth Amendment protection real meaning.

The Supreme Court has been called on to clarify and uphold the Fourth Amendment many times. The Court has defined what is considered a reasonable search and what is not. Police may search a person at the scene of an arrest for a concealed weapon without getting a search warrant. A car may also be searched without a warrant if a police officer has a good reason to be suspicious that a crime has occurred.

In this age of advanced technology, there are many other kinds of searches besides someone physically entering a home or car. Records on everything from our health to our driving are kept on computers and can be accessed by many people. In 1967 the Supreme Court ruled that a court order (or warrant) was required in order for authorities to use electronic devices such as wiretaps (for telephone calls) and bugs (for other conversations). New laws still need to be written to deal with other forms of modern technology.

Due Process

Our system of justice is based on the belief that a person is innocent until proven guilty. The burden of proof is on the accuser, not the accused. All care must be taken to protect the innocent from being falsely prosecuted, by procedures known as due process. Sometimes this means that the guilty go free because their guilt cannot be proven. Our system accepts this as the cost of the protection of the innocent.

The Fifth Amendment details some of the rights of due process. It has several parts. The first states that a person cannot be charged with a serious offense without sufficient evidence. The second part is called the double jeopardy clause, meaning that a person tried and acquitted, or found innocent, cannot be tried again on the same charge, unless the first trial was declared a mistrial or if there was a hung jury (a jury that is unable to come to a verdict).

The next part is probably the most well known, and is the part referred to when someone "takes the Fifth." It states that a person cannot be forced to be a witness against himself or herself. It is popularly known as the right to remain silent. It means that the courts must have evidence beyond what they can force a person to say in order to convict him or her of a crime. The famous *Miranda* ruling of the Supreme Court stated that people taken into custody must be informed of their right to remain silent.

The Sixth, Seventh, and Eighth Amendments deal with the manner in which trials shall be conducted. In the Sixth Amendment, the right to legal assistance, a speedy trial, an impartial jury, and the right to confront one's accusers are declared. The Seventh Amendment deals further with trial by jury.

What exactly is meant by the Eighth Amendment's prohibition of "cruel and unusual punishment" has long been debated. Usually it is interpreted as meaning punishment that is cruel under any circumstances, such as torture, or punishment that is excessive for the crime, such as life imprisonment for a traffic violation. In 1890 the Supreme Court declared that capital punishment (the death penalty) must be carried out as swiftly and painlessly as possible. In 1972 the court declared that capital punishment *as then practiced* in the United States

Due process protects the innocent from being falsely prosecuted. A person cannot be charged with a crime without sufficient evidence, and he or she is presumed innocent until proven guilty.

was cruel and unusual, and thus in violation of the Eighth Amendment. However, in 1976, it held that capital punishment for first degree murder was not *necessarily* unconstitutional; it depends on how it is carried out.

Recent polls seem to indicate that a large number of Americans are in favor of the death penalty. Many believe that it is an appropriate punishment for certain of the most terrible crimes, and that it discourages people from committing these crimes. This is called a deterrent. Others maintain that "virtually every study ever made proves that the death penalty has no effect as a deterrent against capital crimes."[5]

Powers of the People, the States, and the Federal Government

The Ninth Amendment talks about "other rights" that Americans have besides those that are specifically named. Some of these other rights might include the right to live where you please or to choose for yourself where to work.

In 1947 a Supreme Court ruling guaranteed that one of these "other rights" was that of government workers (and others) to participate in politics. The right to privacy is also said to be upheld by the Ninth Amendment.

According to the Tenth Amendment, powers not given to the federal government are reserved for the states and the people. Some of these powers have been determined to include the regulation of marriage, divorce, education, and driver licensing. The states are also able to raise taxes and regulate business within their borders.

However, state laws may not override or be in conflict with federal laws.

From the time that these ten amendments, known collectively as the Bill of Rights, were added to the Constitution, they have been examined and debated. In time, other amendments have been added to the Constitution. We shall look, in the next few chapters, at some of these additional amendments, and at how the constitutionally protected rights of Americans have been shaped, as we look at the ways Americans have fought for their rights.

4

Freedom—for Whom?— 1791–1954

The founding fathers knew that slavery was in conflict with the philosophy of the new government they were creating. But because some of the states were refusing to be part of the nation if slavery was outlawed, it was allowed to continue to exist under the Constitution. The framers apparently decided that it was more important to form the nation first and worry about ending slavery later. "They decided not to deal with what now seems an obvious question: How could a nation that proclaimed the freedom of all people ignore the fact that many people within its borders were not free?"[1]

The Constitution referred to these "unfree people" in Article 4, Section 2 as "persons held to service or labor," but it meant slaves, and the Bill of Rights did not apply to them. They had no rights. Not even their children belonged to them. In fact, after the revolution, free African Americans lost many of the precious few rights that they had maintained before.

Before the revolution, free men of color voted even in the southern colonies. Afterward, they lost this right almost everywhere. . . . A black man could not testify against a white in the courts of California, Illinois, Indiana, Iowa, Ohio. He could not serve on a jury except in Massachusetts. It was seldom possible for him to win a law suit or have a fair trial.[2]

Despite their service in the Revolutionary War, African Americans were now forbidden to serve as soldiers.

Abolition and the Civil War

Right from the start, there were Americans who believed that slavery must be abolished, or brought to an end. By the 1830s the abolitionist movement was gaining attention. One of the greatest abolitionists was Frederick Douglass, a former slave who spoke on behalf of freedom for his people. He pointed out that the philosophy of freedom that the United States was so proud of was not a reality for a large group of its people.

The abolitionist movement was dealt a serious blow in 1857 when the Supreme Court declared in the *Dred Scott* case that African Americans were not citizens entitled to rights under the Constitution.

Then, in 1861, eleven southern states that relied on slaves to labor in the fields declared that they had the right to secede, or leave the United States. The federal government, under the leadership of Abraham Lincoln, thought otherwise, and the Civil War was fought.

At first the North resisted the use of African Americans as soldiers. Then, in September 1862, President Lincoln announced the Emancipation Proclamation, which stated that as of January 1, 1863, all slaves in the

According to the *Dred Scott* decision of 1857, the Bill of Rights did not guarantee African Americans any rights at all. Many African Americans were sold or traded at places like this.

rebellious states "shall be then, thenceforward, and forever free." About the same time, Lincoln finally authorized the first regiments of what were officially called "United States Colored Troops." Besides helping the Northern cause in terms of manpower, these troops also served to disrupt the Southern cause by attracting former slaves and by providing African Americans with the opportunity to fight for their freedom. And fight they did, with more than one hundred eighty thousand African-American soldiers involved by the war's end and some two hundred thousand additional African Americans serving the United States Army as nurses, laborers, and guides.

Reconstruction

At the end of the Civil War, many of the large plantations were taken from their rebel owners. Others were abandoned and wasted. In some places, land was given to former slaves, called freedmen, or to Northerners who had come south.

But old attitudes die hard, and many of the former slave owners could never see the former slaves as anything but inferior beings. "White supremacy" was what they believed in their hearts, and they created laws to keep the freedmen from being truly free. These became known as Black Codes.

Under the Black Codes, marriages between the races were punishable by death. Black ownership of a gun was illegal. Any black man not employed by a white man could be arrested and forced to work on a white-owned farm or business. This was used to disrupt the efforts of blacks who might try to start their own businesses, work their own farms, or attend one of the black colleges that had been opened. The codes were also used to support sharecropping, the South's answer to the end of the plantation system. Under sharecropping, a person worked a portion of a farm owned by someone else. At harvest time, the sharecropper and the landowner split the profits. This sounds fair enough. But somehow when the profits were split, the sharecropper always owed more (for the seeds, tools, and rent on a shack) than his share of the profits. Each year the sharecropper grew more tightly bound to the landowner by debt. Sharecroppers who tried to run away from these debts could be beaten or killed.

In response, Congress passed several new amendments and civil rights acts, and sent federal troops into the South to enforce them. A Freedmen's Bureau was established to assist the former slaves in getting their own land. This period (between 1865 and 1875) became known as Reconstruction. It was a time of hope for the former slaves.

The first of the new amendments after the Civil War was the Thirteenth, officially ending slavery in all of the United States. The Fourteenth Amendment states that the federally guaranteed rights of individuals may not be violated by the states. It also states that all persons born in the United States and subject to its laws, are citizens of the United States. This overruled the 1857 *Dred Scott* decision which declared that African Americans were not citizens. The Fifteenth Amendment declared that the right to vote could not be denied on the basis of race.

In a few places where African Americans were a vast majority, worthy candidates for political office were elected. Seventeen African-American men served in the

United States Congress during Reconstruction. Two more served in the Senate.

Understandably, many African Americans expected that they would enjoy all the civil rights of American citizens. But while Congress was making racial equality the law, the Supreme Court chipped away at its effectiveness. In 1883 the Court declared the Civil Rights Act of 1875, which had outlawed discrimination in public places, unconstitutional.

Groups such as the Ku Klux Klan, which claimed that white people were superior to black people, were formed to intimidate and punish former slaves who appeared to them to be out of line.

And, as time went by, many Northerners lost interest in regulating change in the South. Troops were withdrawn and Reconstruction declared over. As a result, the hard-won civil rights of the newly freed African Americans quickly disappeared.

Though Reconstruction was brief and not without its shortcomings, it was an era that ". . . remains a monument to faith in human equality. The history of these legal strivings to wipe out the incidents and badges of slavery, as well as its roots, and to bring the four million freed Negroes into full membership in the human family, where they could enjoy and suffer the condition of being human equally with white persons, belongs among the noblest pages of the history of mankind."[3]

People Without Rights

With the close of Reconstruction, the northern part of the country was focused on industrialization. "The failures [of the promises] of Reconstruction were an

Groups like the Ku Klux Klan were formed to intimidate former slaves. These hate groups still exist today.

outgrowth of American, not southern, problems. [Many] Northerners no more believed in black equality than Southerners."[4]

Prejudice against various minorities could be found throughout the United States. The Chinese, who had helped build the transcontinental railroad, were seen in the 1870s as a threat to white jobs, and were particularly hated on the West Coast. "The Chinese are inferior to any race God ever made," stated a California legislative report.[5] They were socially segregated and denied political rights.

Mexican Americans would suffer the same fate in the Southwest. Native Americans, once the only residents of the continent, were increasingly losing their land and with it their ability and right to live according to their traditions. "By 1885 the American Indians were a people without rights, privileges, or freedom in their homeland."[6]

Separate and Unequal

As large numbers of African Americans moved into the cities of the North, hoping to escape prejudice, they were forced by unwritten "gentlemen's agreements" among landlords to live in certain neighborhoods which soon became overcrowded and run-down. They certainly had more freedom than preceding generations had as slaves, but they were still a long way from equality.

Meanwhile, women, both black and white, were still denied the right to vote. When a Supreme Court decision (*Minor* v. *Happersett*) said that states' constitutions could set limits on who could vote, the denial of voting rights for women was upheld. This ruling would also be used

A former slave, Frederick Douglass was the leading spokesman for African Americans in the 1800s. He protested segregated seating on trains, used his house as a stop on the Underground Railroad, and discussed the problem of slavery with President Lincoln.

by southern states determined to keep African Americans from voting. Ridiculous tests, outrageous taxes, or sheer violence kept African Americans from voting.

Voting was not the only thing African Americans in the South were not allowed to do. They were forced into separate accommodations on trains, in restaurants, and in virtually all public places—that is, in the places they were allowed to be at all. When a man named Homer Plessy decided to protest this, the Supreme Court declared in *Plessy* v. *Ferguson,* that separate facilities were acceptable, as long as they were equal. This became known as the "separate but equal" doctrine, although the separate facilities were never really equal. Laws that enforced the separation of the races were called Jim Crow laws.

For many African Americans in the South, riding the train was not their primary concern. Many lived in extreme poverty with little reason to hope for a better future. Lynchings—sudden, violent death at the hands of white men—were all too common. According to Ida B. Wells-Barnett, an African-American teacher and journalist, African Americans were being lynched at a rate of two per week in the South between 1890 and 1899, and very often they were African Americans who made the mistake of becoming successful. In 1893 she wrote, "In the past ten years over a thousand black men and women and children have met this violent death at the hands of a white mob. And the rest of America has remained silent."[7]

Another spokesperson for African Americans was Booker T. Washington, founder of Tuskegee Institute,

Ida B. Wells

"I'D RATHER GO DOWN IN HISTORY AS ONE LONE NEGRO WHO DARED TO TELL THE GOVERNMENT THAT IT HAD DONE A DASTARDLY THING THAN TO SAVE MY SKIN BY TAKING BACK WHAT I HAVE SAID." --1917

Ida B. Wells-Barnett (1862–1931) was an outspoken activist for civil rights.

who stressed that education and hard work were the tickets to success.

In contrast to Washington's call for humility, diligence, and patience, another African-American leader, W.E.B. DuBois, told African Americans to "resist . . . agitate . . . resist!"[8] He published a book called *The Souls of Black Folk*, and in 1905 he gathered twenty-nine African-American leaders for a conference that led to the forming of the Niagara Movement. In Harper's Ferry, West Virginia, on August 18, 1906, DuBois said "We claim for ourselves every single right that belongs to a free born American, political, civil, and social."[9]

In 1909 a multiracial group signed a document calling for the rights of African Americans as citizens. This document became the foundation for the group which would be called the National Association for the Advancement of Colored People (NAACP), incorporated in 1910. DuBois was named director and editor of *Crisis*, the official publication of the organization. Also in 1910, the National Urban League was formed to help formerly rural African Americans adjust to urban life in the North.

Yet another African-American leader arose in 1919. He was Marcus Garvey, founder of the Universal Improvement Association. He urged blacks to reject white society and its meager offers of help. He believed in black separatism to the point of an eventual black exodus to Africa. Though tens of thousands supported his organization at its height, Garvey was imprisoned in 1925 then exiled, and the movement fell apart. But its basic philosophy would return again in later years.

The Red Scare

The early 1900s were years in which the face of America was being changed by the arrival of millions of immigrants. Many dealt with prejudice and discrimination as they competed with "older" Americans for jobs and a piece of the good life that America promised. Sometimes those promises were discovered to be half-truths, or even outright lies.

One of the darkest periods for America came during World War I, a war that broke out in Europe in 1914. In 1917, when he declared that the United States would enter the war, President Woodrow Wilson said that it was a war to make the world safe for democracy. However, on the same day that America entered the war, Wilson asked Congress to pass a bill that would punish people for their opinions if they were against the government's judgments. The Espionage Act was signed by the president in June 1917.

> In one stroke, freedom of speech and freedom of the press were crippled in America. Any criticism of the war could be considered a crime. It was not just a question of an *act* of treason or spying. Any *opinion* contrary to the official view could be punished by 20 years in prison.[10]

Some Americans disagreed with this. A man named Norman Thomas wrote a pamphlet called "War's Heretics," which opposed the war and the way the rights of those who opposed it were abused. "Democracy degenerates into mobocracy unless the rights of the minority are respected," he wrote.[11]

The Civil Liberties Bureau was founded in 1917 by a group of people who agreed with Thomas. In 1920 it became the American Civil Liberties Bureau (and later the American Civil Liberties Union, known as the ACLU) under the leadership of Roger Baldwin.

Baldwin and his friends were concerned about protecting the First Amendment right of free speech. The nation was overcome by hysteria and a fear of "the enemy within." A feeling of suspicion was created. Americans were accusing other Americans of disloyalty at a rate of over one thousand reports to the Justice Department each day. The lives of many innocent people, whose only crime was to express an unpopular opinion, were disrupted and in some cases ruined.

After the war, the persecution of people who held unpopular opinions increased, fueled in part by high unemployment and inflation. Almost everything was blamed on Bolsheviks, Russian communists. One of the worst violations of civil liberties in American history occurred with the Palmer raids in 1920. They were named for Attorney General A. Mitchell Palmer, who wanted to be the man to end the "Bolshevik menace." The raids were a series of extremely unreasonable searches and seizures, accompanied by destruction of property and physical brutality. Arrests were made without warrants and individuals were detained for long periods of time without charges being made against them. On one night, January 2, 1920, more than four thousand people were arrested in thirty-three cities.

A New Deal

The Great Depression, after the stock market crashed in 1929, was another period in which attacks on civil rights increased because of economic fears. President

Franklin Roosevelt's New Deal solutions to the nation's economic problems brought some protection of individual rights. But the government also increased its presence in the everyday lives of the American people.

In 1935 the Wagner Act established the National Labor Relations Board (NLRB) and guaranteed American workers the right to organize unions. Unions are groups of workers who join together to improve the salary, working conditions, working hours, and general security of their members. Author Samuel Walker has called the Wagner Act "arguably the greatest civil rights law in American history."[12]

In many quiet ways, African Americans had continued to struggle to claim the promises made to them after the Civil War. In 1934 Arthur W. Mitchell was elected to the House of Representatives from Illinois. He was the first African American in Congress since the Reconstruction. In the 1930s, boycotts of white-owned stores in black communities that refused to hire blacks succeeded in getting a few jobs for blacks. The Congress of Industrial Organizations (CIO) became the first national labor union to include African Americans.

For the people living their day to day lives, however, these improvements were too small and too slow in coming. Life was too hard, and frustration grew. In 1935 some of that frustration exploded in a terrible riot in New York City.

Jobs and the end of economic discrimination were what African Americans needed most. When war broke out again in Europe, labor leader Asa Philip Randolph proposed a March on Washington to protest discrimination against African Americans' involvement in the war effort. On June 25, 1941, Franklin Roosevelt issued Executive Order No. 8802, opening jobs in defense industries to African Americans.[13] When the United States entered World War II, many African Americans participated. Segregation and discrimination, however, still existed.

The 1940s

A number of important civil rights cases were decided during the 1940s. During the height of World War II, the ACLU defended the right of Jehovah's Witnesses not to salute the flag, and the Supreme Court agreed. In the majority opinion for the Court, Justice Robert Jackson wrote, "If there is any fixed star in our constitutional constellation, it is that no official, high or petty, can prescribe what shall be orthodox in politics, nationalism, or other matters of opinion or force citizens to confess by word or act their faith therein."[14] America had come a long way since the hysterical repression of rights during World War I.

One of the most glaring exceptions to this, and a total disregard for civil rights, was the removal of Japanese Americans to internment camps during the war. After the bombing of Pearl Harbor, Japanese Americans and even "anybody who looked Oriental" were subject to harassment, especially in California. Many were fired from jobs, some saw their homes burned, and others suffered beatings.

In 1942 some West Coast politicians and military leaders convinced the Roosevelt administration that "certain persons" should be excluded from certain areas. As a result, one hundred twenty thousand Japanese

One of the most astonishing violations of civil rights in American history took place when people of Japanese descent were taken from their homes and placed in detention centers during World War II.

Americans were put in internment camps (detention centers), for no other reason than their ethnic background. This was a gross violation of their civil liberties. Sadly, this action was upheld by the Supreme Court. (In 1988, the U.S. Congress officially apologized to Japanese Americans and offered to pay twenty thousand dollars to each surviving detainee.)

McCarthyism

As fear of communism grew after World War II, persons accused of being communists, sympathizing with communists, or even just knowing communists, were brought before a special congressional committee and forced to declare their loyalty to the United States or face severe consequences. In the late 1940s and early 1950s, the hearings of this committee turned into a "witch-hunt" as the search for "communist subversives" reached a frenzy. The name of the committee's chairman, Senator Joe McCarthy, was associated first with anticommunism and then later with bullying tactics when his methods became visible after some of the hearings were televised. Finally, in December 1954, the Senate and the country had enough of McCarthy and his wild accusations. The reign of McCarthyism came to an end when the senator was censured, or reprimanded by the Senate.

Separation Is Unequal

After the war there was an investigation into discrimination in the armed services. An important step forward was taken in 1948 when President Truman called for "equality of treatment in the armed service."

Many public places were segregated during the first half of the twentieth century. This movie theater had an entrance for black people, separate from the entrance for white people.

When United States forces fought in Korea from 1950 to 1953, they were integrated, or racially mixed, for the first time in American history. Some African-American officers were given command positions in these integrated troops.

The NAACP fought for these and other civil rights improvements throughout the 1940s and early 1950s. Under the Margold Strategy, named for NAACP lawyer Nathan Margold, civil rights lawyers emphasized the unequal aspects of the "separate but equal" doctrine. The cases of several African-American graduate students showed how unequal the separate facilities really were. When it came time for the Supreme Court to consider several cases of unequal conditions in segregated elementary schools, the NAACP argued that separate facilities were unnecessary, unfair, and unconstitutional.

Five cases were put together and became known as *Brown* v. *Board of Education.* As part of the case, psychologist Dr. Kenneth B. Clark testified that segregation made black children feel inferior. He showed how both black children and white children would choose white dolls to play with, and reject black dolls because they thought white was better.

On May 17, 1954, the Supreme Court voiced its opinion. In the words of Chief Justice Earl Warren: ". . . in the field of pubic education the doctrine of 'separate but equal' has no place. Separate educational facilities are inherently unequal."[15] It was an overturning of the *Plessy* v. *Ferguson* case of 1896, and a major milestone in civil rights. It meant that the wall of segregation, so carefully constructed to keep the races apart, had been cracked at last.

5

Cracks in the Wall— 1954–1965

Many southerners disagreed with the Supreme Court's decision in the *Brown* case. "You are not obliged to obey the decisions of any court which are plainly fraudulent [and based on] sociological considerations," said Mississippi Senator James Eastland.[1] He thought the Supreme Court didn't understand the South. In 1955 the Supreme Court further declared that desegregation, the ending of separate or segregated schools, should proceed "with all deliberate speed." Opposition to the change in black people's status was substantial. White supremacists formed groups called Citizen's Councils to fight desegregation. They tried to control blacks economically and with violence—threatened and real.

During the summer of 1955, a fourteen-year-old Chicago boy named Emmett Till was visiting relatives in a small town in Mississippi. One day he flirted with a married white woman in a local grocery store. Upon leaving the store, Emmett reportedly said, "Bye, baby," to the woman. The next day Emmett Till was dragged from his uncle's home by the woman's husband and another man. A few days later, Emmett's body was pulled from a nearby river. He had been brutally beaten, had a heavy piece of machinery tied to him, and had been shot. Emmett's uncle identified the two men who had dragged Emmett away, knowing that he would then have to move away or he probably would be shot too. One witness said "It was the first time in the history of Mississippi that a Negro had stood in court and pointed his finger at a white man as a killer of a Negro."[2] Still, the all-white jury reached a verdict of not guilty in the murder case.

A Stride Towards Freedom

Later that year, in Montgomery, Alabama, a forty-three-year-old seamstress named Rosa Parks was told to stand up because a white man wanted her seat on a crowded bus. According to local laws, blacks had to sit at the back of the bus while whites sat in the front. There was a middle area where blacks could sit unless whites needed the seat, and that was where Mrs. Parks sat. But Rosa Park's feet were tired and she was protesting against the way blacks were treated by whites. She refused to get up. The driver called the police. Rosa Parks was arrested for breaking the law regarding bus riding in Montgomery, Alabama.

When local leaders of the NAACP found out about what had happened, they decided that the time was right for the African-American people of Montgomery to take a stand.

They called for a boycott of Montgomery's buses for Monday, December 5, 1955. On that day, the buses were nearly empty. African-American citizens met at a local church to decide what to do next. A new organization called the Montgomery Improvement Association was formed to organize a continuation of the boycott. A young minister named Martin Luther King, Jr., was chosen to lead it. ". . . If we protest courageously and with dignity," he said, ". . . future generations will say, 'There lived a great people, a black people, who injected new meaning and dignity into the veins of civilization.'"[3]

Every day for the next year, the city's African-American workers walked, carpooled, and rode African-American-owned taxis to their jobs. The homes of King and others were bombed, and hundreds of protestors were sent to jail for such crimes as "too many passengers in a car" and "conspiracy to boycott." But they remained nonviolent, and in December 1956, the Supreme Court declared that segregation on Montgomery buses was unconstitutional.

African Americans throughout the South began to think that maybe, just maybe, the Supreme Court meant what it said and segregation would have to go. At least, the cracks in the wall were getting wider.

In January 1957 King became the president of a new organization, the Southern Christian Leadership Conference (SCLC). The SCLC was dedicated to bringing about freedom and justice in America through the use of nonviolent protest.

The same year a civil rights act, the first since Reconstruction, was passed. It gave the government the duty to step in when the civil rights of individuals, including the right to attend an integrated school and the right to vote, were threatened.

School districts in border areas between the North and South, such as Missouri, Kansas, and Indiana, quietly integrated without major incidents. But in most of what is known as the Deep South, it was more difficult. Many whites were determined to resist.

The Little Rock Nine

During the spring of 1957, the school board of Central High, a school for white students in Little Rock, Arkansas, was preparing its plan for integration. Nine students from the black junior high and high school were selected to attend Central the following fall.

As the first day of school approached, segregationists, those opposed to multiracial schools, demanded that their governor stop the integration. Governor Faubus responded by calling out the Arkansas National Guard and posting them around the school. When the African-American students tried to go to school, they were yelled at by an angry mob that had gathered, and they were turned away by the soldiers. Not until President Dwight Eisenhower called in the army were the Little Rock Nine, as they students were called, finally able to attend class.

But that was not the end of it. For the rest of the year, the black students at Central put up with the harassment of a small but determined group of white students who threatened them, called them names, knocked down their books, and generally made their

President Eisenhower had to call in the army to ensure that the Little Rock Nine were able to attend school.

lives miserable. The next year Governor Faubus closed all the public schools in Little Rock rather than integrate.

Little Rock was not alone. By 1960, school integration had not even begun in at least five states in the South, and only a few African-American students had been integrated in several others. "On the sixth anniversary of the [*Brown*] decision, only six percent of the South's Negro pupils were attending schools with white pupils."[4] The promises of the *Brown* decision remained largely unfulfilled.

Meanwhile the battle for civil rights was picking up speed, as African Americans began to work for integration of more than just schools.

A Movement Is Born

On February 1, 1960, four young African-American men who attended college in Greensboro, North Carolina stopped in a local Woolworth™ store. The store had no problem taking their money for a few small items they bought, but when they sat down at the lunch counter, they were told that the store would not serve them. The young men were asked to leave but they would not. They remained seated at the lunch counter, without being served, until the store closed.

A few days later, more students joined them. By the end of a week, over three hundred students were demonstrating against segregated lunch counters in Greensboro. The sit-ins, as they were called, spread like wildfire to other cities in the South. Blacks across the country, and some whites too, began to picket outside the stores that

Here, an African-American man enjoys his meal at a lunch counter shortly after integration.

would not serve blacks. In July 1960, the lunch counters in Greensboro were integrated.

In April 1960, students in Nashville, Tennessee, formed an organization called the Student Nonviolent Coordinating Committee (SNCC, pronounced "snick"). The students adopted a code of nonviolence that was inspired by Indian leader Mahatma Gandhi and by SCLC leader Martin Luther King, Jr. Young people from all over America who believed in what was becoming known as "the Movement" joined by the hundreds. "Within the year, over fifty thousand people had demonstrated against segregation in some way."[5] They protested in parks, museums, beaches, libraries, and even churches until the laws of segregation began to come down.

A Ride for Freedom

A civil rights group called the Congress of Racial Equality (CORE), led by James Farmer, had been working to end segregation on interstate buses and trains for some time. The Supreme Court had declared that form of segregation illegal in 1946, but it was still widely practiced in the South.

In May 1961, CORE leaders organized what they called the Freedom Rides. Together, black and white protestors intended to ride interstate buses from Washington, D.C., through Alabama and Mississippi to Louisiana. They would not obey the local rules for segregated seating on the buses or in the rest rooms and waiting areas of the terminals, because they believed that these rules were unconstitutional.

In the Alabama towns of Anniston, Birmingham, and Montgomery, Freedom Riders became victims of some of the most brutal violence of the civil rights movement. Even a government official, sent by Attorney General Robert Kennedy to investigate, was beaten by the angry mob. More volunteers poured into the South, determined to take a bus ride for freedom.

In November 1961, the Interstate Commerce Commission declared that it would comply with the Supreme Court ruling that had made segregation in interstate bus and train travel illegal.

A Heavy Price

In the fall of 1962, a twenty-nine-year-old veteran named James Meredith was registered to attend the University of Mississippi at Oxford, Mississippi. A violent mob gathered on the campus to protest because Meredith was black, and the student body at "Ole Miss" had always been white. As President John Kennedy was speaking on television from Washington, D.C., urging people to accept integration peacefully, two men were killed and many others injured because of rioting by the mob. Federal troops were called to the campus to restore order and escort James Meredith to class.

In April 1963, Martin Luther King, Jr., went to Birmingham, Alabama, to participate in a protest against segregation. George Wallace, the governor of Alabama, had said that there would be "no integration in Alabama—ever!"[6] When SCLC leaders led a protest march on Good Friday, April 12, they were promptly arrested. From his cell King wrote an essay entitled "Letter from a Birmingham Jail." In it he explained why African Americans could wait no longer for equality.

"We have waited for more than 340 years for our constitutional and God-given rights," he said.[7]

On May 2, another march was held in Birmingham. Nine hundred protestors were arrested. When twenty-five thousand people marched the next day, police chief "Bull" Connor had powerful fire hoses and brutal attack dogs turned on the crowd. Two days later, three thousand people marched. This time, many of the policemen refused to obey Connor's orders to attack the marchers. Protestors kept marching, until finally Birmingham businesspeople, concerned about empty stores, pleaded with city officials for a settlement. When white supremacists heard that Birmingham was to be desegregated, they went on a bombing and looting spree.

As if crowded jails and attack dogs weren't enough, two murders in 1963 further dramatized the dangers of fighting segregation in the South. On April 23, 1963, William L. Moore, a white Baltimore postman, was shot in northeastern Alabama. Moore had been attempting to walk from Tennessee to Mississippi carrying a sign saying "Equal Rights for ALL—Mississippi or bust." His body was found on a road.

On June 12, 1963, Medgar Evers, an African-American man, was shot in the driveway of his home as he was returning late at night from his work as NAACP state chairman in Jackson, Mississippi. His wife, waiting for him inside, heard his car door slam, and then heard the shots that took his life.

One week later, President Kennedy sent a civil rights bill to Congress. "It ought to be possible for American consumers of any color to receive equal service in places of public accommodation, such as hotels and restaurants, and theaters and retail stores, without being forced to resort to demonstrations in the streets," the president said.[8] The president's words might seem somewhat weak today, in view of the fact that people were being killed because of the color of their skin.

"I Have a Dream"

On August 28, over two hundred fifty thousand people came to Washington to march for jobs and freedom. One hundred years had passed since President Lincoln had issued the Emancipation Proclamation during the Civil War. The descendants of slaves were still not treated as equal citizens in America. Black unemployment was twice that of whites, and the average income for a white family was nearly double that of a black family.

In the shadow of the Lincoln Memorial, a number of civil rights leaders addressed the crowd of protestors. One was Asa Philip Randolph, who had threatened a march on Washington when Franklin Roosevelt was president. Another was Martin Luther King, Jr., who gave one of the most famous speeches of his career.

"I have a dream . . ." King said. "I have a dream that one day . . . little black boys and black girls will be able to join hands with little white boys and white girls as sisters and brothers."[9]

The March was called ". . . the largest and most peaceful demonstration that the capital had ever seen."[10] It was a day for dreams, a day for hope.

But a few weeks later, on September 15, a bomb exploded in the Sixteenth Avenue Baptist Church in Birmingham, and four young girls attending Sunday

On August 28, 1963, Martin Luther King, Jr., (front row, first from left) spoke at the March on Washington for equality and civil rights for people of all races.

school were killed. Two young African-American men were also killed in Birmingham that day, one by the police and one by a mob. Dreams and hopes it seemed were fragile things.

A Different Opinion

Meanwhile, ten thousand African Americans held a separate meeting in Washington, D.C. They were Black Muslims, members of a religious organization known as the Nation of Islam. Their leader was a small man named Elijah Muhammad, and his right-hand man was an individual known as Malcolm X. Many of their followers were from the inner city and had found an alternative to a life of crime and desperation in the strict behavior codes of the Nation of Islam. Members did not drink alcohol or use drugs, and they dressed neatly and acted with moral discipline. They had a different opinion as to how to handle the problem of injustice against African Americans in the United States. As a group, they believed in racial separation, not integration. They told African Americans to be proud of who they were and to defend themselves in any way necessary. Their membership was relatively small compared to the major civil rights organizations, but their message was quite strong.

Taking the Message to Mississippi

On November 22, President Kennedy was killed. Lyndon Johnson, the new president, told the nation that its greatest tribute would be acceptance of the civil rights act that Kennedy had worked for. Congress passed this act in 1964. Lyndon Johnson also outlined programs to make "war on poverty." Many people had come to believe that civil rights issues and economic issues were closely tied.

One of the places where this was dramatically apparent was in rural Mississippi. During the summer of 1964, a massive voter registration drive was organized there. The project was named Freedom Summer. The Student Nonviolent Coordinating Committee trained volunteers, black and white, mostly college students, mainly from the North, to work in the rural areas of Mississippi, registering black voters.

Almost immediately, three volunteers disappeared. Andrew Goodman and Michael Schwerner were white, James Chaney was black. As federal authorities searched for the missing volunteers, hundreds of others were arrested by local law enforcement officers, and some were beaten. Homes and churches of Mississippi's African-American citizens were burned and bombed. In August the bodies of Goodman, Schwerner, and Chaney were found in an earth-filled dam.

But out of Freedom Summer came the Freedom Democratic Party (FDP), organized to show the determination of African-American citizens to vote and participate in the democratic process. Delegates from the FDP went to Atlantic City, New Jersey, where the Democratic party's convention was being held, stating that they had received more votes in their districts than the regular Democratic party's candidates. They were not seated at the convention, but they gained national attention for their cause.

The national program known as Head Start, designed to assist disadvantaged preschool children of all races, was also an outgrowth of both Freedom Summer and the war on poverty, as were several other federal assistance programs. For both the poor sharecroppers of Mississippi and the volunteers who had come to help them, life would never be quite the same again. The wall that had been segregation crumpled a little more.

Selma, Alabama

Despite all the protests and marches, and the promises of the Civil Rights Acts of 1957 and 1964, African Americans were still not enjoying their rights as citizens in many places in the South. "In Selma, Alabama, there were only 355 blacks registered to vote out of fifteen thousand who were eligible. Martin Luther King, Jr., and other civil rights leaders planned a march from

Selma to [the state capital in] Montgomery to dramatize the problem."[11]

When they tried to march from a church to the courthouse in Selma on Monday, February 1, 1965, hundreds were arrested and sent to jail. The protest continued, and on March 7 marchers began the planned walk to Montgomery. On a bridge on the outskirts of Selma, police, some mounted on horses and others armed with cattle prods and whips, charged the marchers. This abuse by the police was televised. "The entire nation now understood the reign of terror by which southern bigots kept blacks from voting."[12] While the protesters regrouped in Selma, a white minister from Boston who had come to participate in the march was beaten to death by a white supremacist mob. On March 15, President Lyndon Johnson sent a voting rights bill to Congress. Using the words that had become a theme of the Movement, he said, "we *shall* overcome."[13] He also sent army troops to Selma to protect the protestors who had permission to make the march to Montgomery.

Americans from all over the country who wanted to show their support of the marchers gathered in Alabama. They were black and white, young and old, and included rabbis, priests, nuns, nurses, lawyers, maids, and miners. Some who had never marched before now joined the Movement by marching from Selma. By the time the marchers arrived in Montgomery, some twenty-five thousand people had participated.

On March 25, Martin Luther King, Jr., presented the marchers' demands on the stops of the state capitol. "We are on the move now," he said, "and no wave of racism can stop us." The petition he presented read, in part, "We have come not only 5 days and 50 miles, but we have come from 3 centuries of suffering and hardship. We have come . . . to declare that we must have our freedom now. We must have the right to vote; we must have equal protection of the law and an end to police brutality."[14]

The Voting Rights Act was signed into law on August 6, 1965.

What the Movement Meant

The march from Selma to Montgomery was one of the last major events of the nonviolent direct-action campaign for civil rights known as the Movement. At about this time there were so many differences in the groups involved, and in the opinions on tactics, that "the Movement" broke up into many movements. This does

Martin Luther King, Jr., helped organize a march from Selma to Montgomery, Alabama, in order to dramatize the problem of too few African-American registered voters.

not mean that the fight for civil rights ended at this time, only that its focus broadened in many ways.

The civil rights movement of the early Sixties did not end injustice in America. But it did bring an end to Jim Crow laws—the legalized segregation of the races for the purpose of treating African Americans in an inferior manner. It also gave African Americans and other minorities tools to use in shaping further change. For many people, the civil rights movement provided their first opportunity to become political—to realize that there was something they could do to change things and hopefully to make things better.

6

The Movement Fragments—1965–1968

The civil rights movement of the early Sixties had challenged American institutions and inspired groups such as students, prisoners, lesbians and gay men, and ethnic minorities to demand that their complaints be heard. Millions of people across America demanded fair treatment and justice. With so many different groups of people with varying needs, it was only natural that the civil rights movement would break up into many movements. "[T]he movement seemed to take on a life of its own and certainly was not a movement that could be controlled by one man or organization."[1]

Among African-American civil rights activists, there were many opinions about what needed to be done next, for whom, and by what tactics. While most of Martin Luther King's followers were working-class African Americans primarily living in the South, Malcolm X gave voice to African Americans caught in the cycles of poverty and despair in the ghettos of the North. In

1964, Malcolm X had split with the Nation of Islam and founded Muslim Mosque, Inc., and, a short while later, the Organization of African-American Unity. He urged his followers to take what was rightfully theirs—their economic and civil rights.

Fires and riots began to break out increasingly in the ghettos, and were seen as symptoms of the hopelessness and frustration of their residents. For example, riots broke out in Harlem on July 18, 1964, when a black teenager was shot by a white off-duty policeman. Other cities in the New York area also experienced riots that summer, as did ghetto neighborhoods in Chicago and Philadelphia.

After a trip to Africa in which he witnessed a spirit of brotherhood between black and white Muslims, Malcolm X modified his basic philosophy. Despite numerous threats on his life, he continued to speak about his programs for improving African-American communities. His work ended, though, on a Sunday afternoon in February 1965, when he was assassinated at a community meeting in Harlem. Many African Americans would continue to follow the teachings of the various Black Muslim groups. After the death of Elijah Muhammad in 1975, several splinter groups broke off, some choosing to embrace more traditional Islamic teachings. Louis Farrakhan became the leader of the faction most closely aligned with the Nation of Islam teachings of Elijah Muhammad. His teachings have been the center of great controversy.

A Burning Rage

There was a great deal of anger and frustration among the poor in the inner cities of the United States. In one inner-city neighborhood, known as the Watts section of

Malcolm X gave a voice to African Americans caught in the cycles of poverty and despair in the North.

Los Angeles, the spark that set off an explosion of rage was a fight between a white police officer and a black youth in August 1965. For five days the streets of Watts were filled with looting and burning.

Thousands of police officers and National Guard troops were used to restore order to the city. Thirty-four people were killed, hundreds were injured, and property damage estimates ranged from $40 to $200 million.

In those few days, it was said that the violence in Watts canceled out much of the goodwill that had been growing between the races due to the nonviolence of the civil rights movement. But the violence spoke dramatically of what African-American writer and activist Bayard Rustin called ". . . the despair and hatred that continues to brew in the Northern ghettos despite the civil rights legislation. . . ."[2]

In an effort to deal with the problems of the northern ghettos, Martin Luther King, Jr., visited Chicago in July 1966. He put a young member of the Chicago chapter of the SCLC, Jesse Jackson, in charge of Operation Breadbasket, the organization's economic program. Jackson would go on to organize a successful boycott of businesses that profited from African-American consumers but would not employ them.

Along with fighting poverty, King began to speak out against the war that the United States was fighting in the southeast Asian nation of Vietnam. He said, "we have been repeatedly faced with the cruel irony of watching Negro and white boys on TV screens as they kill and die together for a nation that has been unable to seat them together in the same schools."[3] He also said,

As racial tensions grew, some African-American leaders became frustrated with the nonviolent civil rights movement.

"The bombs in Vietnam explode at home. They destroy the hopes and possibilities of a decent America."[4]

The war in Vietnam, inner-city poverty, and continued resistance to integration and voting rights in the South led some African-American leaders to grow frustrated with the nonviolent movement. There were some (especially among college students and young adults) who lost patience with King and the supporters of nonviolence. They were tired of getting beaten up while playing by the rules. They wanted more than desegregation. They wanted power and they wanted it now. They suggested that racism was so deeply imbedded in American society that it was hopeless to attack it law by law.

James Meredith, the young man who had been the object of anger when he attended classes at Ole Miss in 1962, decided in the spring of 1966 to march from the Tennessee/Mississippi border to Jackson, Mississippi, in a protest against fear. On June 6, as he walked along a Mississippi highway, he was shot and wounded by a sniper in a bush. Members of a number of civil rights groups, including Stokely Carmichael, leader of SNCC; Floyd McKissick of CORE; and Martin Luther King, Jr., of SCLC decided to continue the march.

As the marchers walked, they encouraged the African-American people of Mississippi to exercise their right to vote. "The march stimulated the registration of about 4,000 Mississippi Negroes and involved at least 10,000 Negroes as temporary participants."[5] Along the way, some of the marchers were beaten, tear gassed, and arrested. Among them was Stokely Carmichael. When he was released, he said, "Never again will I take a

President Lyndon B. Johnson signed the Civil Rights Act on July 2, 1964. The law guaranteed equal job opportunities for all, and opened all public businesses to African Americans.

beating without hitting back! We been saying freedom for six years, and we ain't got nothin'. What we gonna start saying now is black power."[6]

More and more this became the rallying cry of the more aggressive civil rights leaders. "We want our rights, NOW, Power to the People!" they shouted.[7] H. Rap Brown, who followed Carmichael as leader of SNCC and was even more militant, warned that if African Americans didn't get their share of America, they would ". . . burn America down."[8] There were riots in Detroit, New York, and, after an H. Rap Brown speech in Cambridge, Maryland, on July 25, 1967, there was a riot there.

President Johnson appointed a group called the Kerner Commission to study the cause of the riots. "We are moving toward two separate societies," the commission reported, "one black and one white—separate and unequal."[9] They cited improvements in housing, education, and employment as necessary to improve conditions for African Americans.

Many of the civil rights leaders realized that racism and poverty were intertwined. A vote meant little, if all of the good jobs and opportunities for success were blocked. This applied to the poor of any color or ethnic background.

While attempting to help striking sanitation workers in Memphis, Tennessee, Martin Luther King was assassinated on April 4, 1968. Riots broke out across the country. There were fires and beatings and thousands of soldiers were called upon to help police restore order. From that time on, the civil rights movement would be increasingly fragmented.

7

Rights for All

Throughout American history there have been many struggles for rights. With the success of the direct-action civil rights movement in bringing down the segregation laws, other groups, including women, Native Americans, and people with handicaps, became more vocal and organized in their demands for recognition of their rights. Since the 1970s, hundreds of cases concerned with various forms of discrimination and other infringements of rights have been tried in the American judicial system.

Women's Rights

Although women are not a minority group, since they make up roughly half of the population of citizens in the United States, they have had many of the same problems in having their rights respected that various minority groups have had. "One definition of 'minority' is people who are socially excluded, economically oppressed, and politically powerless. Using that definition, women make up the largest minority in America."[1]

In 1848 a group of women gathered in Seneca Falls, New York. At this convention, they delivered their own declaration of independence. "We hold these truths to be self-evident that all men and women are created equal," they said.[2] They expressed their determination to fight for legal rights, including the right to own property, the right to educational opportunities, and greater opportunities in employment.

The Fourteenth Amendment, added to the Constitution after the Civil War, clearly gave women rights as citizens (since it used the word "persons" instead of "men"). Women expected that the Fifteenth Amendment, which would be a voting rights amendment, would use the same words, but it did not. It said that the right to vote could not be withheld on the basis of race, but did not mention gender. Many women were angry and disappointed. Susan B. Anthony, a leader in the fight for women's rights, registered and voted in the 1872 election, and was promptly arrested for it. She gave a powerful speech in response, asking "Is it a crime for a United States citizen to vote?"[3]

In 1869 Wyoming became the first state to allow women to vote, and over the following decades several other western states followed. In 1913 Illinois became the first state east of the Mississippi to grant women the vote. By 1917, with many women working to support the war effort in World War I, eleven states had given them the right to vote, and a woman (Jeannette Rankin

Women were not guaranteed the right to vote until the Nineteenth Amendment was ratified in 1920.

from Montana) was elected to the United States House of Representatives. The Nineteenth Amendment, which made it illegal to bar the right to vote on the basis of gender, became law on August 26, 1920, giving women the right to vote.

After that, the women's movement went into hibernation and was not revived in an organized way until the 1960s. At that time, many women who had participated in the movement for African-American rights felt that it was time to speak up for women's rights as well.

A 1963 book called *The Feminine Mystique*, written by Betty Friedan, challenged the traditional roles that society had for women. In 1966, Friedan helped found the National Organization for Women (NOW) to establish "full equality for all women in America in truly equal partnership with men, now."[4]

The idea of an Equal Rights Amendment (ERA), to assure women the full rights of citizenship, was revived. (A similar amendment had been proposed in the 1920s but was met with little support.) This time many women and a number of rights groups, including the ACLU, supported it. Others were concerned that it would require treating women exactly like men, including drafting them into the army, and even eliminating separate public rest rooms.

In 1979 the ERA had been accepted in thirty-four states, with thirty-seven needed for ratification. With the deadline extended to 1982, passage seemed assured. But then a Stop-ERA movement was organized and was successful in blocking ratification in key remaining states. The ERA was never passed.

This defeat did not mark the end of the women's rights movement, but rather a shift in tactics. Women chose to fight their battles for rights through laws and courts, and in the workplace. Women continue to be concerned with employment opportunities and legal rights.

The issue of reproductive rights has also been very important for women. In 1973, in a case known as *Roe v. Wade*, the Supreme Court ruled that women have the legal right to choose whether to have a child or have an abortion without government interference in what could be considered a private decision. Ever since this decision was made, abortion opponents have fought against it. They have succeeded in having a number of laws passed that place restrictions on the right to an abortion. And they continue to fight, hoping to one day make virtually all abortions illegal.

Some of the goals of the women's movement have been achieved. For example, women have been hired in many positions that had formerly been exclusively male. The fact remains, though, that women generally earn less than men for doing identical work, and millions of American women are not well off. Many of the social programs that helped the families of poor and working women have been cut since the early 1980s. Some experts predict that by the year 2000 all poor people in America either will be women or children.[5]

Protections for Children

Throughout most of American history, children have worked at difficult and dangerous jobs for low pay. For a long time there were no limitations on the age at which children could be sent to work or on the authority of parents over their children. Children as young as nine worked twelve to fourteen hour days in factories and mines. They worked for less pay than adults and often in the most dangerous positions.

In the early 1900s, reformers began to work for laws that would protect children. A child labor law signed by President Franklin Roosevelt protected young children from being forced to work. Since then, the rights of children have been examined and reevaluated throughout the years.

Many people feel that children have some special rights, such as rights to an education and to economic support. In America, when children are accused of breaking the law, they are tried in juvenile courts where their age is a major factor in determining what happens to them.

There are also some rights that adults have that children are denied—including the right purchase certain products such as alcohol, and the right to get married.

The government sponsors programs like Head Start, which serves disadvantaged preschool-aged children, in an effort to help them. But as of 1990, only about 20 percent of eligible children were being served.[6]

In an editorial in March 1995, Marion Wright Edelman, head of the Children's Defense Fund, responded to Congress's proposed cuts of benefits to children saying, "How does hurting innocent children and their struggling families achieve Congress's goals of reducing bureaucracy, putting people to work and improving our children's education? . . . Each and every one of us should worry about this shameful assault on children. A nation that mistreats its poor and disabled children jeopardizes and devalues all its children and its economic and democratic future."[7]

In 1990, the United Nations sponsored a World Summit for children. "Out of it came the International Convention on the Rights of the Child, a fifty-four-article document that adds children to the ranks of those whose human rights must be protected by their governments."[8] One of the freedoms the charter proclaims is the right to "freedom of thought, conscience, and religion." Some organizations and individuals feel that this threatens the parents' rights to bring up their children in the religion or value system of their choice.

The Convention of the Rights of the Child has been ratified by more than one hundred countries, but, so far, not by the United States. It is proving to be a tricky and complicated matter to provide for the rights of children without infringing on the rights of good parents.

Things can be pretty complicated when it comes to the rights of students as well. Young adults and school officials are both protected by the United States Constitution. Sometimes, however, their rights are in conflict. For example, if school officials have what is considered a reasonable suspicion of wrongdoing, they may search a student's desk, locker, or personal belongings. In this case, the right of the school to maintain order outweighs the student's personal privacy rights.

Students' rights to free speech are similarly limited. The Supreme Court determined in 1969 that students could not be punished for wearing black armbands to school in protest of the Vietnam War. This kind of "symbolic" speech is protected. But if the school can

In the past, there were no laws protecting the rights of children. Often, they were forced to work at difficult and dangerous jobs for low pay. Today, people argue that some laws protecting children's rights interfere with parents' rights to raise their children without government interference.

prove that certain types of speech "materially and substantially" disrupt schoolwork (such as shouting in the halls), or violate the rights of others (such as verbally abusing a teacher), such activities can be prohibited and can lead to punishment.

Native Americans

When Europeans began to settle along the Atlantic seaboard and in the dry Southwest in the early 1600s, there were between one and three million people already in the region that is now the United States according to estimates. There were about two hundred fifty tribal groups with unique civilizations and a variety of lifestyles. They negotiated treaties with the well-armed newcomers, and the relationship was like that between two independent nations.

"After the Revolutionary War, the new American nation signed treaties with the Indian nations and followed a policy toward them as they would toward any foreign country." In 1787, part of the Northwest Ordinance stated that the Indian nations' "lands and property shall never be taken from them without their consent; and, in their property, rights, and liberty, they shall never be invaded or disturbed. . . ."[9]

However, one by one the tribes were forced to sign away more and more of their land. In 1830 the Indian Removal Act forced many thousands of Native Americans in the eastern half of the country to follow what they later called the Trail of Tears to land beyond the Mississippi River. This land in what was then called Indian

Territory was considered to be reserved for them, which is how the term reservation was created. As more and more whites headed to the West, Indian Territory grew smaller and smaller, and the Native Americans of the West were forced to live on reservations too.

Life on reservations was hard. Much of the land was unfit for farming. Native Americans on reservations were forced into a lifestyle that made them dependent on the United States government. Also, they were not considered citizens until 1924. Now, most Native Americans on reservations are considered both citizens of their tribes and of the United States, and are governed by a combination of federal, state, and tribal law, and by various court decisions.

In the 1960s, inspired by African Americans' advances in civil rights, Native Americans renewed their struggle for their rights as well. In 1973 some members of a group called the American Indian Movement (AIM) seized some buildings in the village of Wounded Knee, South Dakota, the site of the murder of 250 Sioux by United States soldiers in 1890. The AIM members demanded an investigation of the Bureau of Indian Affairs and insisted that Americans in general take note of the conditions of poverty in which so many Native Americans lived.

In 1976, the Indian Self-Determination Act encouraged Native Americans to take control of their finances and education. The federal government seemed ready to admit that perhaps assimilation into white culture wasn't the only answer to Native Americans' problems, and that Native Americans had a right to preserve their own traditions and languages.

Even today, most Native Americans in this country (and especially many of those living on reservations) can be described as very poor. "The life expectancy in some tribes is just forty-five years, and Indians have both the highest unemployment rate and the lowest per capita income of any ethnic group in the U.S."[10]

In some places, backlash groups have formed that protest what they see as special rights granted to Native Americans. South Dakotans for Civil Liberties is one, and the Interstate Congress of Equal Rights and Responsibilities (ICERR) is another. In a hearing before the United States Commission on Civil Rights in 1977, an ICERR member said, "We seek just one thing, that is equal rights for all people living under the Constitution of the United States and the Fourteenth Amendment . . . [which] gives equal rights for all people. . . ."[11] The United States Supreme Court has tended to interpret the Constitution as defining Native American tribes as governments with whom the United States has treaties, thus justifying certain special policies.

For many Native Americans, life is a blending of old ways and new as they seek to make the most of their rights as America's first people, and as American citizens.

Hispanic Americans

Hispanic and Latino are words that describe people of Spanish-speaking heritage in the United States.

> Spanish-speaking peoples constitute the largest non-English-speaking minority in the United States today. . . . Some can trace their ancestry on U.S. soil as far back as the sixteenth century. Others arrived

just last year. Some hail from Mexico, some from Puerto Rico, some from Cuba, some from Central America. Many are farm laborers and unskilled workers; many others are professionals and entrepreneurs.[12]

Many of the Spanish-speaking people in America have come from Mexico, and they often provide leadership in the struggle for rights among Hispanics. Cesar Chavez, a migrant farm worker, tried to improve the working and living conditions for Mexican Americans in the 1960s, starting with California grape pickers. When the wealthy vineyard owners responded with threats and harassment, Chavez led the harvesters out on strike. Fellow Americans were asked to show their support by boycotting grapes and certain products made from California grapes, like particular wines. By the 1970s the grape pickers and other migrants were aided by the United Farm Workers Union.

Some groups of Mexican Americans call themselves "Chicanos." They tend to want to retain many aspects of their Mexican-American heritage, including the Spanish language. The Bilingual Education Act of 1968 provided federal funds for bilingual education and was supported by a 1974 Supreme Court ruling. *Lau* v. *Nichols* stated that without the act, children with a limited knowledge of English could not receive equal treatment in schools.

In 1965 a Mexican American from Colorado, Rodolfo Gonzales, founded the Crusade for Justice, an organization that tried to provide social services and job opportunities for Mexican Americans. Poverty and discrimination make it difficult for many Mexican Americans to participate in the political process. In

1990, 25 percent of Mexican Americans remained below the poverty level.[13] "Continuing serious efforts need to be made to eliminate stereotyping and racial stigma and to open the American system wider to Mexican Americans and other minorities."[14]

Today's Immigrants

The United States government was founded by immigrants and the descendants of immigrants who arrived during the seventeenth and eighteenth centuries, mostly from England and other northwestern European countries. During the early 1900s, laws were written to restrict immigration from various parts of the world. These laws were obviously discriminatory.

In 1965 President Johnson signed an Immigration Act that sought to improve the situation. Since that time, the number of immigrants from Asia, Central America, and South America has greatly increased. In 1980, the Refugee Act made it easier for people fleeing overly powerful or violent governments to enter the United States. The Immigration Reform and Control Act of 1986 allowed thousands of individuals illegally living and working in the United States to receive legal status.

Many of today's immigrants come from countries with very different economic, social, and political conditions than those of the United States. They must learn the way things work in America, and often they face very difficult struggles to have their human as well as civil rights honored.

Other Groups

There are many groups of people who have benefited from an increased awareness of the civil rights of American citizens.

One such group is made up of Americans with disabilities. A bill called the Rehabilitation Act of 1973 has been called the Bill of Rights for people with disabilities. It prohibits discrimination of persons with disabilities by any program that receives federal assistance. Reserved parking spaces and ramps at the entrances to public buildings were some of the results of this legislation.

This act was further strengthened in 1990 when President Bush signed into law the Americans with Disabilities Act. Some say it is the most sweeping civil rights law since the 1964 Civil Rights Act. It presents new employment opportunities and greater access to public accommodations, transportation, and virtually all aspects of life for people with disabilities.

Another case of a special situation is that of residents of low-income housing complexes known as projects. Currently there is debate over whether or not police should be able to conduct unannounced, warrantless searches known as "sweeps" in the projects, looking for guns, drugs, and gang activities. Supporters say that such drastic measures are necessary to protect the children and law-abiding citizens who live there from gangs and other criminals. They say that the war-zone conditions of the projects make such searches "reasonable," and therefore acceptable according to the Fourth Amendment. But the American Civil Liberties Union leads the ranks of those who protest. First of all, they say, these raids don't work—they do little to improve security in the buildings.

Besides that, they add, the searches are in violation of Fourth Amendment rights.

About the only thing that is clear in all these different situations is that the determination of rights is a complicated business requiring both background knowledge and problem-solving skills.

8

Today, Tomorrow, and . . . One Day

Today there are many laws that protect the civil rights of American citizens. These laws were written as a result of the actions of individuals who had the courage to stand up and say to fellow citizens and to the government, "you can't do that to me." Does that mean that civil rights as an issue is a thing of the past? Definitely not.

In 1987, a young black man named Michael Griffith was killed in New York when he was chased into the path of an oncoming car by five white teenagers. In 1988, in New York City alone, over two hundred incidents of violent racial occurrences were reported. At about the same time, *The New York Times* reported that crimes directed against minorities were on the rise among young people.[1] People who call themselves skinheads have been charged with deliberately starting racial incidents.

No, the need for an awareness of civil rights is far from over, and it is likely that it never will be. Even if we could conquer racism and terrorism, we would still need to be aware of just what our rights are, in order to keep them protected.

The Rainbow Coalition

In 1988, longtime African-American activist Jesse Jackson ran a significant campaign for the Democratic party's presidential nomination. He spoke for the African-American underclass living in the inner-city ghettos. Many of them found themselves unemployed as a great number of manufacturing jobs were either eliminated or moved out of the cities. Many of the economic gains achieved by African Americans as a result of the civil rights movement in the 1960s had been wiped out by the conservative financial practices of the 1980s.

But Jesse Jackson spoke not only to and for African Americans. "He talked about the struggles of women, still earning 60 percent of what men earn; about Hispanics, who used to be ashamed to talk in Spanish; about the gay community, urging people to have compassion for people with AIDS; about the disabled; the disadvantaged; the farmers."[2] He referred to the diversity of his supporters as a "Rainbow Coalition."

Jackson was defeated in his bid for the nomination by Michael Dukakis, who was in turn defeated by the Republican candidate, George Bush. During the campaign, Bush called Dukakis "a card-carrying member of the ACLU," implying that belonging to a major civil rights organization was a crime.[3]

Ironically, the ACLU would defend Bush's right to make that remark, for it believes that "every view, no

During his 1988 bid for the presidency, Jesse Jackson spoke on behalf of African Americans, women, Hispanics, homosexuals, and people with disabilities. He called the diversity of his supporters the Rainbow Coalition.

matter how ignorant or harmful we may regard it, had a legal and moral right to be heard."[4] They have even defended free speech for those who oppose free speech. (Neither communists nor Ku Klux Klan members advocate free speech, but the free speech rights of those groups have been supported by the ACLU.) As founder Roger Baldwin maintained, "The only test for our integrity of purpose is our willingness to defend persons with whom we totally disagree."[5]

This is a valuable point to consider. Too many Americans have fallen under the spell of "my freedom—yes; your freedom—no." The majority has all too often, all too viciously, suppressed ideas it did not like.

As individuals, people have a right to boycott or otherwise express their opposition to books, movies, statements, or other things they do not like or do not agree with. But when that opposition goes so far as to impose their will on other peoples' ideas, they have entered into censorship and perhaps violations of the freedom of speech of others. People have the right to protest when they believe that the government has violated their rights. They do not have the right to blow up a building in which hundreds of other people are going about their business—as was the case in Oklahoma City in April 1995.

We struggle with the question of reverse discrimination—what some people call the preferential treatment sometimes given to women and minorities to compensate for past discrimination. Those who support affirmative action (policies aimed at increasing the number of people from certain social groups in employment, education, business, government, and other areas) defend it as necessary to achieve a level

These two men protested a Ku Klux Klan rally. It is important to note that *all* citizens have the right to assemble—from the KKK to civil rights activists.

playing field in which the disadvantages of minorities are compensated for. They point to advances in higher education and employment made by women and minorities that would have been much less likely without special protections. Others claim that each individual should be judged solely on their qualifications, without special consideration of circumstances. They say that affirmative action discriminates against people who don't happen to be members of a minority. Many people agree that affirmative action has helped individuals who might otherwise have been discriminated against in the past. There is considerable debate however, as to whether or not the time has come to end this policy of deliberately taking race into account to help people.

There are many laws that attempt to safeguard the rights and liberties of American citizens. But it takes informed citizens, willing to participate in the democratic process. You have to know your rights in order to fight for them. You have to vote for representatives who will respect your rights.

We need to learn from the lessons of history, to balance the desires of the majority with the protection of minorities, to balance concern for public safety with individual rights. We have to know what our rights are in order to know when they are being violated. We have to know how to go about dealing with this. We need to learn from the Palmer raids, the McCarthy hearings, the lunch-counter sit-ins, and the Freedom Rides.

On March 3, 1991, a black man named Rodney King was brutally beaten by white Los Angeles police officers after being stopped for a traffic violation. A bystander with a video camera recorded the incident,

97

and the police officers were brought to trial. When the jury declared them innocent in May 1992, several neighborhoods in Los Angeles erupted into the most violent rioting in years.

In 1993, an African-American professor at Princeton University named Cornel West published a book called *Race Matters.* In it he described some of the frustrations of African Americans. He told of how he once stood on a corner in New York City and waited while nine taxis passed him by and the tenth stopped only to pick up "a smiling female citizen of European descent."[6] It was just one of many times he was treated as an inferior simply because of the color of his skin, and it is an experience similar to that of many African Americans.

On October 3, 1995, Americans listened spellbound as the verdict was read in the trial of O.J. Simpson, former football star and actor, accused of murdering his ex-wife and her friend. The case had focused attention on the different ways people are treated in American society depending on what categories they fall into: rich or poor, male or female, black or white. When the jury announced that they found Simpson not guilty, many people reacted according to what category *they* fit into. Many whites believed that Simpson was guilty, and were shocked by the verdict. Many blacks did not believe that the prosecution had proved its case against Simpson, especially considering that one of the police investigators was clearly prejudiced against African Americans. Women were concerned that the wrong message would be sent to men who use violence against their wives. And many people wondered if Simpson's wealth had been the deciding factor in winning his freedom. It was painfully obvious that there were still many divisions within American society. After nearly three decades, the issues raised by the Kerner Commission remain unresolved.

On October 16, 1995, another event highlighted those divisions. This time it was the Million Man March, organized by Nation of Islam leader Louis Farrakhan in an attempt to encourage African-American men to take greater responsibility for their lives, their families, and their communities. Hundreds of thousands of African-American men attended, and many brought their sons.

For some, the march inspired memories of the crowd that had gathered at the same spot in the shadow of the Washington Monument in August of 1963. On that day Martin Luther King, Jr., had talked of his dreams. Thirty-two years later there had been some headway in fulfilling some of those dreams. For others, the march was a symbol of the racial and religious prejudices of its leader, Louis Farrakhan. America remains a place where people of all races, religions, and ethnic backgrounds need to be aware of what their rights and responsibilities are, and learn how to make sure they are protected.

Chronology

1774, **October 14**—The American colonies issue a Declaration of Rights, asserting that they are no longer bound by the British Parliament or king.

1787, **May 25**—Delegates from the states meet in Philadelphia to revise the Articles of Confederation, and end up writing the Constitution.

1791, **December 15**—The first ten amendments, known as the Bill of Rights, become part of the Constitution.

1830—The Indian Removal Act forces thousands of Native Americans to move to reservations in the West.

1848—A group of women meet in Seneca Falls, New York to demand legal rights.

1865, **December 6**—The Thirteenth Amendment abolishes slavery. The Supreme Court declares in *Plessy* v. *Ferguson* that "separate but equal" treatment is acceptable.

1905, **July**—W.E.B. DuBois meets advocates of African-American rights and begins the Niagara Movement, which will lead to the creation of the NAACP in 1910.

1917—The Civil Liberties Bureau is founded, which will become the American Civil Liberties Union (ACLU).

1920, **January 2**—Four thousand people are arrested in cities across the country in the Palmer raids.

1920, **August 26**—The Nineteenth Amendment gives women the right to vote.

1935—The Wagner Act established the National Labor Relations Board and gives workers the right to form unions.

1942—One hundred twenty thousand Japanese Americans are forced to move to "detention centers."

1954, May 17—The Supreme Court decides the *Brown* v. *Board of Education* case in favor of desegregating schools.

1954, December—Joe McCarthy is censured by the Senate, thus ending the period known as McCarthyism.

1955–1956, December—African-American citizens of Montgomery, Alabama, boycott the buses of their city until their demands for desegregation are met.

1957, September—Federal troops escort nine African-American high school students to class in Little Rock, Arkansas.

1960, February 1—College students in Greensboro, North Carolina, begin a sit-in at a drugstore which ignites a grassroots desegregation movement around the country.

1961, May—Freedom Riders are beaten and arrested in Alabama.

1963, April—Martin Luther King, Jr., is jailed during a protest in Birmingham, Alabama.

1963, August 28—Two hundred fifty thousand people gather in Washington, D.C., for a March for Jobs and Freedom.

1964—President Johnson signs the Civil Rights Act President Kennedy had sent to Congress the year before.

1965, **February 21**—African-American activist Malcolm X is assassinated.

1965, **March 25**—Protesters reach the steps of the state capitol in Montgomery, Alabama, after marching from Selma to protest restrictions on voting rights.

1965, **August**—Devastating riots destroy much of the Watts area of Los Angeles, California.

1965, **August 6**—The Voting Rights Act becomes law.

1966, **June**—Some African-American leaders, including Stokely Carmichael, begin calling for "black power."

1967—Kerner Commission reports "two separate societies."

1968, **April 4**—Martin Luther King, Jr., is assassinated.

1960's—Cesar Chavez leads migrant workers on a strike against California grape-growers and forms the United Farm Workers Union.

1973—Members of the American Indian Movement protest for Indian rights at Wounded Knee, South Dakota.

1988—African-American leader Jesse Jackson runs for Democratic presidential nomination, supported by a "Rainbow Coalition."

1990—President Bush signs Americans with Disabilities Act, guaranteeing access to public places for people with handicaps.

1995—O.J. Simpson trial and acquittal leads Americans to reexamine issues of racism and rights.

Chapter Notes

Chapter 1

1. Richard Lacayo, "A Moment of Silence," *Time*, May 8, 1995, p. 45.

2. Ibid., p. 46.

3. Ibid., p. 46; Judith Smolowe, "Enemies of the State," *Time*, May 8, 1995, p. 60.

Chapter 2

1. Reginald Wilson, *Think About Our Rights: Civil Liberties and the United States* (New York: Walker & Company, 1988), p. 1.

2. John A. Garraty, *The American Nation: A History of the United States* (Harper & Row, 1966), p. 133.

3. *1791–1991, The Bill of Rights and Beyond* (Washington, D.C.: Commission on the Bicentennial of the United States Constitution, 1991), p. 6.

4. Harold Faber and Doris Faber *We the People: The Story of the United States Constitution since 1787* (New York: Simon & Schuster Children's, 1987), p. 82.

Chapter 3

1. James Finn and Leonard R. Sussman, eds., *Today's American: How Free?* (New York: Freedom House, 1986), p. 142.

2. Julie S. Bach, ed., *Civil Liberties: Opposing Viewpoints* (St. Paul, MN: Greenhaven Press, 1988), p. 50.

3. John A. Garraty, *The American Nation: A History of the United States* (New York: Harper & Row, 1966), p. 169.

4. Milton Meltzer, *The Bill of Rights: How We Got It and What It Means* (New York: Thomas Y. Crowell, 1990), p. 115.

5. Ibid., p. 148.

Chapter 4

1. Walter Dean Myers, *Now Is Your Time: The African American Struggle for Freedom* (New York: HarperTrophy, 1991), p. 67.

2. Dorothy Sterling, *Tear Down the Walls: A History of the American Civil Rights Movement* (Garden City, N.Y.: Doubleday, 1968), p. 48.

3. Milton R. Konvitz, *A Century of Civil Rights* (New York: Columbia University Press, 1961), p. 65.

4. William Loren Katz, *Reconstruction and National Growth, 1865–1900* (New York: Franklin Watts, 1974), p. 71.

5. Patricia and Fredrick McKissack, *The Civil Rights Movement in America from 1865 to the Present* (Chicago: Children's Press, 1991), p. 71.

6. Ibid., p. 74.

7. Myers, p. 212.

8. McKissack, p. 82.

9. Sterling, p. 117.

10. Roberta Strauss Feuerlight, *America's Reign of Terror: World War I, the Red Scare and the Palmer Raids* (New York: Random House, 1971), p. 34.

11. Samuel Walker, *In Defense of American Liberties: A History of the ACLU* (New York: Oxford University Press, 1990), p. 12.

12. Ibid., p. 101.

13. McKissack, p. 84.

14. Walker, p. 109.

15. Juan Williams, *Eyes on the Prize: America's Civil Rights Years, 1954–1965* (New York: Viking Penguin, 1987), p. 34.

Chapter 5

1. Juan Williams, *Eyes on the Prize: America's Civil Rights Years, 1954–1965* (New York: Viking Penguin 1987), p. 38.

2. Ibid., p. 48.

3. Pete Seeger and Bob Reiser, *Everybody Says Freedom* (New York: W.W. Norton & Company, 1989), p. 17.

4. Milton R. Konvitz, *A Century of Civil Rights* (New York: Columbia University Press, 1961), p. 131.

5. Patricia and Fredrick McKissack, *The Civil Rights Movement in America from 1865 to the Present* (Chicago: Children's Press, 1991), p. 209.

6. Ibid., p. 217.

7. Williams, p. 188.

8. McKissack, p. 221.

9. Williams, p. 205.

10. Dorothy Sterling, *Tear Down the Walls: A History of the American Civil Rights Movement* (Garden City, N.Y.: Doubleday, 1968), p. 206.

11. McKissack, p. 244.

12. Williams, p. 265.

13. Ibid., p. 278.

14. Lester A. Sobel, ed., *Civil Rights 1960–1966* (New York: Facts on File, 1967), p. 303.

Chapter 6

1. James Haskins and Kathleen Benson, *The 60s Reader* (New York: Viking Kestrel, 1988), p. 34.

2. Bayard Rustin, *Down the Line* (Chicago: Quadrangle Books, 1971), p. 140.

3. Patricia and Fredrick McKissack, *The Civil Rights Movement in America from 1865 to the Present* (Chicago: Children's Press, 1991), p. 250.

4. Harvard Sitkoff, *The Struggle for Black Equality 1954–1980* (New York: Hill and Wang, 1981), p. 219.

5. Lester A. Sobel, ed., *Civil Rights 1960–1966,* (New York: Facts on File, 1967), p. 393.

6. McKissack, p. 254.

7. Ibid., p. 255.

8. Sitkoff, p. 217.

9. Anna Kosof, *The Civil Rights Movement and Its Legacy* (New York: Franklin Watts, 1989), p. 16.

Chapter 7

1. Patricia and Fredrick McKissack, *The Civil Rights Movement in America from 1865 to the Present* (Chicago: Children's Press, 1991), p. 275.

2. *1791–1991: The Bill of Rights and Beyond* (Washington, D.C.: Commission on the Bicentennial of the United States Constitution, 1991), p. 72.

3. Rheta Childe Dorr, *Susan B. Anthony: The Woman Who Changed the Mind of a Nation* (New York: AMS Press, 1970), p. 255.

4. Anna Kosof, *The Civil Rights Movement and Its Legacy,* (New York: Franklin Watts, 1989), p. 70.

5. Charles W. Eagles, ed., *The Civil Rights Movement in America,* (Jackson: University of Mississippi Press, 1986), p. 143.

6. McKissack, p. 291.

7. Marian Wright Edelman, "Her Say," *Chicago Tribune,* March 19, 1995, Section 6, p. 8.

8. McKissack, p. 292.

9. Judith Harlan, *American Indians Today: Issues and Conflicts* (New York: Franklin Watts, 1987), p. 14.

10. Reginald Wilson, *Think About Our Rights: Civil Liberties and the United States* (New York: Walker & Co., 1988), pp. 30–31.

11. Harlan, p. 51.

12. McKissack, p. 302.

13. Matt S. Meier and Feliciano Ribera, *Mexican Americans/American Mexicans: From Conquistadors to Chicanos* (New York: Hill and Wang, 1993), p. 257.

14. Ibid., p. 273.

Chapter 8

1. Anna Kosof, *The Civil Rights Movement and Its Legacy*, (New York: Franklin Watts, 1989), p. 80.

2. Ibid., p. 102.

3. Samuel Walker, *In Defense of American Liberties: A History of the ACLU* (New York: Oxford University Press, 1990), p. 3.

4. Ibid., p. 62.

5. Ibid., p. 64.

6. Cornel West, *Race Matters*, (Boston: Beacon Press, 1993), p. x.

Glossary

affirmative action—The effort to overcome past discrimination by increasing the number of people from certain social groups in employment, education, business, government, and other areas.

assimilation—The process of being made similar. Many minorities have been encouraged to assimilate, or become similar, to the rest of society.

backlash—A negative reaction to something. Backlash rights groups protest that civil rights advocates of one group interfere with the rights of another.

boycott—To refrain from buying or doing something as a means of protest. For example, during the civil rights movement, people boycotted companies that sold products to the African-American community but would not hire African Americans.

discrimination—Treating individuals in a negative manner due to the color of their skin, their ethnic background, or a similar consideration.

due process—A system for dealing with accused people in a fair and just manner.

federal—Relating to the United States government, as opposed to state or local governments.

habeas corpus—A right that means that you can only be imprisoned by authorities if you are justly charged with a crime.

infringe—To violate or disregard; an infringement of your rights is something that violates or disregards your rights.

integration—To bring together into the same group or area, as in integrating people of different races.

majority—The group having the most of something, such as power, usually due to the number of people involved.

militant—Behavior that suggests aggression or a readiness to fight.

minority—A subgroup of a larger group which is different from the rest, and usually smaller in number than the rest.

picket—To protest against something outside a building, such as unfair employment practices at a business, usually by carrying signs expressing dissatisfaction.

prejudice—Negatively prejudging individuals on the basis of race, ethnic background, or similar considerations. Most prejudice turns out to be based on false beliefs or information.

ratification—The act of accepting or agreeing upon something. Amendments to the Constitution must be ratified.

Further Reading

Faber, Doris, and Harold Faber. *We the People: The Story of the United States Constitution Since 1787.* New York: Charles Scribner's Sons, 1987.

Hanmer, Trudy J. *Affirmative Action: Opportunity for All?* Hillside, N.J.: Enslow Publishers, 1993.

Kosof, Anna. *The Civil Rights Movement and Its Legacy.* New York: Franklin Watts, 1989.

Kronenwetter, Michael. *Under 18: Knowing Your Rights.* Hillside, N.J.: Enslow Publishers, 1993.

McKissack, Patricia, and Fredrick McKissack. *The Civil Rights Movement in America from 1865 to the Present.* Chicago: Children's Press, 1991.

Meltzer, Milton. *The Bill of Rights: How We Got It and What It Means.* New York: Thomas Y. Crowell, 1990.

Sterling, Dorothy. *Tear Down the Walls: A History of the American Civil Rights Movement.* Garden City, N.Y.: Doubleday & Company, Inc., 1968.

Williams, Juan. *Eyes on the Prize: America's Civil Rights Years, 1954–1965.* New York: Viking Penguin, Inc. 1987.

Wilson, Reginald. *Think About Our Rights: Civil Liberties and the United States.* New York: Walker and Co., 1988.

Index

A

Adams, President John, 21
affirmative action, 5, 95, 97
Alien and Sedition Acts, 20-21
American Civil Liberties Union
    (ACLU), 45, 47, 80, 90, 93,
    95
American Indian Movement
    (AIM), 86
Americans with Disabilities Act
    (ADA), 90
Anthony, Susan B., 78

B

Bill of Rights, 10, 14, 16-17, 20,
    31, 32
Black Codes, 35
black power, 76
Brown, H. Rap, 76
Brown v. *Board of Education,* 51,
    52, 57
Bush, President George, 90, 93

C

capital punishment, 28, 30
Carmichael, Stokely, 74, 76
Chavez, Cesar, 88
civil rights
    defined, 9
    limits on, 10, 19, 21, 44, 83, 95
    and African Americans, 10,
        14, 32-33, 35-37, 39, 41,
        43, 46, 47, 51-55, 57,
        59-70, 72, 74, 76, 93, 98,
        99
    and children, 81-83
    and Chinese Americans, 39
    and immigrants, 21, 89
    and Japanese Americans, 10,
        47, 49
    and Mexican Americans, 39,
        88, 89
    and Native Americans, 39,
        77, 85-87
    and persons with disabilities,
        90, 93
    and students, 83
    and women, 39, 77-78,
        80-81, 93
Civil Rights Acts, 37, 54, 61, 64,
    65, 90
Clinton, President Bill, 6
Constitution, the United States,
    5, 10, 13-14, 16-21, 23,
    25-28, 30-33, 36, 37, 61,
    78, 80, 83, 87, 90, 91
    the First Amendment, 18-21,
        23, 45
    the Second Amendment, 23,
        25
    the Third Amendment, 23, 26
    the Fourth Amendment, 26,
        27, 90, 91
    the Fifth Amendment, 27-28
    the Sixth Amendment, 28
    the Seventh Amendment, 28
    the Eighth Amendment, 26,
        28, 30
    the Ninth Amendment, 30
    the Tenth Amendment, 30
    the Thirteenth Amendment,
        36
    the Fourteenth Amendment,
        36, 78, 87
    the Fifteenth Amendment,
        36, 78
    the Nineteenth Amendment,
        80
Congress of Racial Equality,
    (CORE), 59

D

Douglass, Frederick, 33
Dred Scott case, 33, 36
DuBois, W.E.B., 43

E

Eisenhower, President Dwight, 55
Equal Rights Amendment, 80
Espionage Act, 44

F

Farrakhan, Louis, 70, 99
Freedom Rides, 59, 97
Freedom Summer, 64, 65
Friedan, Betty, 80

G

Gandhi, Mahatma, 59
Garvey, Marcus, 43

H

Head Start, 65, 82

J

Jackson, Jesse, 72, 93
Jim Crow laws, 41, 68
Johnson, President Lyndon, 64,
  66, 76, 89

K

Kennedy, President John, 60, 61,
  64
Kennedy, Robert, 60
Kerner Commission, 76, 99
King, Martin Luther Jr., 54,
  59-63, 65-67, 69, 72, 74,
  76, 99
Ku Klux Klan, 37, 95

L

Lincoln, President Abraham, 33,
  35, 62
Little Rock Nine, 55

M

Malcolm X, 63, 69-70
March on Washington, 46, 62,
  63, 99
McCarthyism, 49, 97
Meredith, James, 60, 74
Movement, the, 57, 59, 66-69,
  72, 74, 76, 77
Muhammed, Elijah, 63, 70

N

National Association for the
  Advancement of Colored
  People (NAACP), 43, 51,
  53, 61
National Organization for
  Women (NOW), 80
Nation of Islam, 63, 70, 99

P

Palmer Raids, 45, 97
Parks, Rosa, 53
Plessy v. *Ferguson,* 41, 51

R

Rainbow Coalition, 93
Randolph, Asa Philip, 46, 62
Roe v. *Wade,* 81
Roosevelt, President Franklin, 46,
  47, 62, 82

S

Selma, Alabama, 65-67
Seneca Falls Convention, 78
sit-ins, 57, 97
Southern Christian Leadership
  Conference (SCLC), 54, 59,
  60, 74
Student Nonviolent
  Coordinating Committee
  (SNCC), 59, 64, 74, 76
symbolic expression, 21, 23, 83

T

Truman, President Harry, 49

V

voting rights, 33, 36, 39, 41, 55,
  64-67, 74, 76, 78, 80, 97

W

Wagner Act, 46
Washington, Booker T., 41, 43
Wells-Barnett, Ida B., 41
Wilson, President Woodrow, 44